Rollin'

Racing Cars

by Jeff Savage

CAPSTONE PRESS
MANKATO

W

C A P S T O N E   P R E S S
818 North Willow Street • Mankato, MN 56001

Printed in the United States of America.

Library of Congress Cataloging-in-Publication Data
Savage, Jeff, 1961-
　　Racing cars / Jeff Savage.
　　p. cm.
　　Includes bibliographical references (p. 46) and index.
　　Summary: Describes some popular race cars and discusses some of the races in which they compete.
　　ISBN 1-56065-368-X
　　1. Automobiles, Racing--Juvenile literature. [1. Automobiles, Racing. 2. Automobile racing.] I. Title.
TL236.S3 1996
796.7'2--dc20

95-43219
CIP
AC

Photo credits
Archive Photos: 8-14
Steve Mohlenkamp: 4-6, 16-43

Table of Contents

Chapter 1 Speed 5

Chapter 2 History 9

Chapter 3 Safety.. 17

Chapter 4 Stock Cars................................... 21

Chapter 5 Indy Cars 27

Chapter 6 Formula 1 Cars 33

Chapter 7 Other Race Cars..................... 39

Glossary 44

To Learn More.. 46

Useful Addresses 47

Index 48

Words in **boldface** type in the text are defined in the Glossary in the back of this book.

Chapter 1

Speed

Car makers have always wanted to see who could build the fastest car. Drivers have always wanted to see who could drive the fastest. So automobile races were created. Special cars were built just for racing.

Many races are held today and many types of race cars are built. Thousands of drivers compete against each other every week.

Most races are local, without much **fanfare**. A few races, though, draw special interest. They are the races in which the best drivers in the world compete for major prizes.

Today's race cars are high-tech machines designed with computers.

The Cars

All race cars share certain elements. They are colorful. They have smooth bodies. They have oversized tires and powerful engines. Three popular types of race cars are stock cars, Indy cars, and Formula 1 cars.

Today's race cars are high-tech machines designed by experts with computers. They are far different from the original race cars, which were built a century ago.

Stock cars, Indy cars, and Formula 1 cars are not the only kinds of race cars. Some other race cars are sprint cars, rally cars, sports cars, and Trans-Am cars.

Chapter 2

History

One of the first organized automobile races took place in 1895 on the open roads of France. The winner was Emile Levassor. He drove a Panhard automobile for 48 hours nonstop. The two-day race was 750 miles (1,200 kilometers) long, from Paris to Bordeaux and back. Levassor's car reached a top speed of 18.5 miles (30 kilometers) per hour.

At the time, races in buggies or on horseback were common. But races in a machine were new. People were fascinated.

In early race cars, a mechanic rode next to the driver.

A New Top Speed

Automobile designers were determined to make their machines go faster. Five years after Levassor's win, another French driver won a race from Paris to Lyon. His name was Fernand Charron. He tinkered with the car's engine to make his car go an average speed of 38.6 miles (62 kilometers) per hour. It reached a top speed of 50 miles (80 kilometers) per hour.

By 1908, it was common to see race cars going down dusty roads at 100 miles (161 kilometers) per hour.

Early Race Cars

Early race cars were different from today's models. The driver's small seat was high off the ground. The driver had to climb a ladder to reach it. Cars did not have windshields or roofs.

The driver wore a helmet and goggles to protect against dust and flying **debris**. Drivers often crashed because they could not see where they were going.

The first Grand Prix was held in 1906 at Le Mans, France.

Large engines were mounted on **rickety** frames. Brakes were simple. Tires were made of solid rubber. They wore out often.

A mechanic rode in a lower seat next to the driver. He made repairs on the automobile when necessary. He watched for traffic, too.

The First Race on a Course

The first automobile race on a racing course was held in 1896. It took place at Narragansett Park in Providence, Rhode Island. The race did not draw worldwide attention.

American race promoters built a special course so fans could see all of a race. The course was called an **oval**.

The track was short with banked turns. Fans could sit in the **grandstands** and watch the cars go around the track. Ovals are still popular today.

Modern Racing

The first **Grand Prix** race was held 10 years later, in 1906. It was held in France, in the city of Le Mans. Grand Prix means great prize in French.

The winner of the race was a Hungarian named Ferenc Szisz. He drove a Renault to a top speed of 100 miles (161 kilometers) per hour.

North American race promoters invented the oval track.

The track at Indianapolis is known as the Brickyard.

The French Grand Prix course was about eight miles (13 kilometers) long. A stretch of road was built just for the race. Thousands of fans gathered at the finish line to see the world's fastest cars.

The Indy 500

The Indianapolis Motor Speedway was built in 1909. The track was 2.5 miles (four kilometers) long with four banked turns. Two years later, the first Indy 500 race was held. The distance of the race was 500 miles (800 kilometers).

A man named Ray Harroun entered the race with a car called the Marmon Wasp. He insisted that he did not need a mechanic to ride with him. Other drivers complained that he would not be able to watch for traffic coming up behind him. So Harroun installed a mirror in his car. It was the first rearview mirror.

Harroun won the race. The Marmon Wasp traveled at an average speed of 74.6 miles (119 kilometers) per hour. The Indy 500 was an instant success.

Speeds Improve

In the 1930s, the British Bentley won many races. So did French and Italian cars like the Maserati, the Bugatti, and the Alfa Romeo. By the end of the decade, the German Mercedes could go 200 miles (320 kilometers) per hour. It was hard to beat.

Race cars were divided into classes after World War II (1939-1945). Among the types of race cars still competing today are stock cars, Indy cars, and Formula 1 cars.

Chapter 3

Safety

Race cars travel at very high speeds. So they are made with special safety devices not found in regular cars.

All race cars have either a **roll bar** or a **roll cage** that surround the driver. These are made from strong metal tubes. If the car crashes, the roll bar or roll cage will prevent the driver from being crushed.

All race cars have elaborate seat belt systems. Drivers are harnessed tight so they cannot be thrown from their cars in a crash. The seat belt keeps the driver within the protection of the car's roll cage or roll bar.

A race car driver is well protected from injuries.

In Case of Fire

After a crash, chances are good that a fire will break out. To protect their bodies, drivers wear fire-resistant clothing and helmets. A fire extinguisher is always within a driver's reach, too.

On Indy cars, a fire extinguisher is set off automatically when a crash occurs. Indy car wheels are made to fall off in a crash. Without wheels, the car will slide rather than roll. Sliding reduces the chance that the driver will be hurt. Indy cars cannot carry more than 40 gallons (152 liters) of fuel. With less fuel, there is less chance of fire.

Stock car bodies are made to absorb crashes. Special materials take the shock first in a crash. The driver is well protected from injuries.

Race car drivers are surrounded by a roll cage or a roll bar which will protect them if they crash.

Chapter 4
Stock Cars

Stock car racing is the biggest motor sport in North America. A stock car looks like it came straight from the factory. Stock cars are modified **sedans** and **coupes**. They look like ordinary family cars but they are not ordinary at all.

A stock car is built strictly for racing. It has a powerful motor. Its body is made of fiberglass instead of metal. The body is reinforced with steel to hold up better in a crash.

The most famous stock car event is the Daytona 500 at Daytona Beach, Florida.

The Beginning

Stock car racing began in the 1930s as an inexpensive form of auto racing. The races were held on dirt tracks or on beaches. Sometimes more than 100 cars entered one race.

Some people say that stock cars were first built by **bootleggers** during the **Prohibition era** (1920-1933). The bootleggers hid alcoholic beverages in ordinary-looking cars that could out-race police cars.

Daytona Beach

Since the early 1900s, such car enthusiasts as Henry Ford had attempted to set land speed records on the hard-packed sand at Daytona Beach, Florida. But in the 1930s, the drivers left Daytona for the Bonneville Salt Flats in Utah.

Daytona officials found a way to keep racing alive in their community. They staged America's first big stock car race in 1936. It was a 250-mile (400-kilometer) race around a 3.2-mile (five-kilometer) oval track.

Stock car racing is more popular in the United States than anywhere else in the world.

In the first race, 28 cars competed for a $5,000 prize. Milt Marion won the race in a Ford. Bill France was Marion's mechanic. France also raced. He finished fifth.

NASCAR

Bill France saw a big future for stock car racing. After World War II, he organized the National Association for Stock Car Auto Racing (NASCAR). He was elected its president.

NASCAR promoted 85 races in 1948, its first year. The following year it promoted 395 races. Drivers won $64,000 in prize money in 1948. Three years later, they won $750,000.

Stocks in the United States

Stock car racing is more popular in the United States than anywhere else in the world. Most races are held on the super speedways of the South.

The most famous event is the Daytona 500 at Daytona Beach, Florida. Other popular oval tracks are at North Wilkesboro in North

Stock car bodies are made of fiberglass.

Carolina, at Darlington Beach in South Carolina, and at Watkins Glen in New York.

Modern Stock Races

NASCAR features a series of races for its top drivers. Until the 1980s, it was called the Grand National Series. It is known today as the Winston Cup Series. Drivers earn points at weekly races around the country. The driver with the most points at the end of the series is the Winston Cup champion.

Chapter 5
Indy Cars

The Indianapolis 500 attracts more fans than any other one-day sporting event in North America. It is held in Indianapolis, Indiana, every Memorial Day weekend.

The Indianapolis track was once paved with bricks. It is known as the Brickyard. Since 1911, when the first race was held there, many types of cars have raced at the Brickyard. All of these cars are known as Indy cars.

The Beginning

Europeans built the first successful Indy cars. But World War I (1914-1918) drained

Indy cars use a fuel called nitromethane.

Today's Indy car is low and sleek.

resources in Europe. So American car designers stepped in.

Harry Miller was a famous designer from Los Angeles. In 1922, Miller created a car to challenge the European cars. The Miller car won the Indianapolis 500.

A year later, Miller built the first single-seat race car. He named it the Miller 122. Its slender body became the Indy look for years to come. Seven Miller 122s were driven in the 1923 race. Miller's cars finished first, second, third, and fourth.

Superchargers

Superchargers were developed during World War I to improve the performance of airplanes. Superchargers pump vaporized fuel into **combustion chambers** where the fuel is ignited.

In 1924, two Indy cars were fitted with supercharged engines. One of the supercharged cars broke a gear. The other car won the race. Harry Miller noticed. In 1925, he supercharged the Miller 122. For the rest of the decade, Miller's supercharged cars dominated the Indy 500.

The Offy

Then the **Great Depression** (1929-1941) hit. Harry Miller went bankrupt. Fred Offenhauser was a mechanic who had worked for Miller. He designed a smaller engine that became known as the Offy. For the next 40 years, almost all winning Indy cars were powered by Offy engines.

Turbochargers

In the 1970s, the engine power of Indy cars was greatly increased with the use of **turbochargers**. A turbocharger has a small fan called a **turbine**. The turbine is turned by exhaust fumes. The turbine drives a **compressor** that forces fuel into the engine.

By 1989, turbochargers were banned at most tracks. They are still allowed at the Brickyard, though.

Modern Indy Cars

Today's Indy car is low and sleek. An open cockpit holds a single seat. The driver sits close to the ground. The engine is behind the driver.

On the back of the race car is a wide piece of fiberglass called an **airfoil**. Air rushes over the airfoil and pushes down on the rear of the car. The pressure keeps the car from lifting into the air and flipping over.

Indy cars use fuel called **nitromethane**. Nitromethane is a mixture of gasoline and alcohol. It is similar to jet fuel.

Turbocharger cars are still allowed at the Brickyard.

Chapter 6
Formula 1 Cars

Grand Prix racing is more popular in Europe than anywhere else in the world. Grand Prix race cars are called Formula cars. They must be built to specific sizes and weights.

Formula 1 is the most popular type of Formula car. There are also Formula 2, Formula 3, and Formula Ford cars. The organization that decides the sizes and weights for each formula is called the Federation Internationale de l'Automobile (FIA).

Grand Prix racing is more popular in Europe than anywhere else in the world.

Formula 1 racing attracts the best drivers in the world.

The Beginning

The World Championship for Drivers in Grand Prix was created in 1950. In this contest, drivers were awarded points for performance in seven races. The races were the Belgian Grand Prix, the British Grand Prix, the ACF Grand Prix, the Italian Grand Prix, the Monaco Grand Prix, the Swiss Grand Prix, and the Indy 500.

Designers

When the World Championship began the fastest Formula 1 cars were Alfa Romeos, Maseratis, Talbots, and Ferraris. Soon, British Racing Motors joined the competition.

In 1951, Alfa laced its gasoline fuel with alcohol. Mercedes joined in, followed by Vanwall. In 1958, fuel mixtures were temporarily outlawed. Formula 1 cars now use nitromethane, the fuel that is used in Indy cars.

In the mid-1950s, Charles Cooper and his son, John, designed a car with the engine behind the driver. This design became the standard for the modern Formula 1 car. By 1959, Cooper cars won eight of the 13 international races they entered.

Modern Formula 1 Cars

Formula 1 racing attracts the best designers and drivers in the world. The top Formula 1 designers today are Renault, Lotus, McLaren, Cosworth, and Ferrari.

Formula 1 cars are similar in many ways. The engine cannot be larger than three liters.

The steering wheel is small. The handling is very sensitive. The tires are wide.

All Formula 1 models feature a **monocoque** design. In North America, this is often referred to as unibody construction. In the monocoque design the body and the **chassis** are all one piece.

Popular Races

Millions of people attend Formula 1 races in Europe every year. It is the most popular form of racing outside the United States. The road courses are usually between 150 and 200 miles long.

The most popular Grand Prix race is held each summer on the streets of Monte Carlo in Monaco. The cars go as fast as 200 miles (320 kilometers) per hour on the straight parts of the track. They may slow down to 30 miles (48 kilometers) per hour on the tight corners.

Formula 1 cars must be built to specific sizes and weights. The organization that decides the sizes and weights is called the Federation Internationale de l'Automobile.

Chapter 7

Other Race Cars

Stock cars, Indy cars, and Formula 1 cars are not the only kinds of race cars. Some other race cars are sprint cars, rally cars, sports cars, and Trans-Am cars.

Sprint Cars

Sprint cars have not changed much since they were first made in the 1920s. They are smaller than most other race cars. The engine is mounted in front of the driver. The driver sits high.

At Le Mans, the car wins the race, not the team.

Tracks for sprint car racing are short. They are usually one-half mile (.8 kilometers) long dirt tracks.

The back of a sprint car slides out around the corners. The cars go almost sideways, kicking up dirt and dust with their tires. The best sprint car drivers race on the World of Outlaws circuit.

Rally Cars

Rally car races are called rallies. They take place in sections. Each section is timed. Drivers lose points if they arrive too early or too late. Rallies can last as long as a week. Some sections of the race are on paved roads. Some are on dirt roads. Some go through forests.

Rally cars are regular cars made to handle the difficult conditions of a rally. They are made to be strong and light. The tires have to work on both pavement and dirt.

Rally cars have both a driver and a navigator. The navigator reads the map and directs the driver. Rally racers have to worry

Sports cars have two seat and covered wheels.

about the weather. They might have to drive
through snow and ice or summer heat and rain.

Sports Cars

Sports cars have two seats and covered
wheels. They have headlights and windshield
wipers. They are driven in long races.

Sports cars are driven by teams of two to
five people. The team members take turns

The most popular Trans-Am cars are the Pontiac Trans-Am, the Chevrolet Camaro, and the Ford Mustang.

driving. The winner is the team that drives the most miles in 24 hours.

The most famous sports car races are Le Mans and Daytona. Drivers at Le Mans cover more than 1,000 miles (1,600 kilometers) before the race is over. Because the course is not as difficult at Daytona, the drivers will cover more than 2,500 miles (4,000 kilometers). At Le Mans, the car wins the race, not the team.

Trans-Am Cars

Trans-Am stands for Trans-American. Trans-Am cars are familiar road cars with standard street engines. The most popular Trans-Am cars are the Pontiac Trans-Am, the Chevrolet Camaro, and the Ford Mustang.

Trans-Am events are usually about 100 miles (160 kilometers) long. They are held on road courses throughout the United States. Each year, there are 14 races in the Trans-Am Championship circuit.

Sports cars are driven by teams of two to five people.

Glossary

airfoil—piece of fiberglass on the rear of a car that prevents it from lifting off the ground

bootlegger—someone who makes, sells, or carries illegal liquor

chassis—the frame of the car on which the body rests

combustion chamber—an enclosed space where fuel is ignited

compressor—a device in a turbocharger that forces fuel into an engine

coupe—two-door car smaller than a sedan

debris—bits, pieces, and fragments of stone, wood, glass, and other materials

fanfare—noisy or showy display

grandstand—seating structure for viewers at an event

Grand Prix—car race popular in Europe. It means great prize in French.

Great Depression—the period of economic hardship that began in 1929 and lasted through 1941

monocoque—a car design in which the body and frame are one piece

nitromethane—mixture of gasoline and alcohol used as fuel

oval—race track that looks like an oblong circle

rickety—likely to break down, shake, or fall apart

Prohibition era—period during which the manufacture and sale of alcoholic beverages was illegal in the United States (1920-1933)

roll cage—on stock cars, tubes welded together that surround the driver and protect against injury

roll bar—on Indy and Formula 1 cars, tubes welded together that protect the driver against injury. A main tube is situated over the driver's head.

sedan—car with two or four doors and posts between the front and rear windows

supercharger—system that pumps vaporized fuel to make a car go faster

turbine—small fan that drives a compressor in a turbocharger

turbocharger—system that forces fuel through an engine to make a car go faster

To Learn More

Barrett, Norman. *Race Cars*. New York: Franklin Watts, 1987.

Dregni, Michael. *Stock Car Racing*. Minneapolis: Capstone Press, 1994.

Fields, Alice. *Racing Cars*. New York: Franklin Watts, 1981.

Rendall, Ivan. *The Power and the Glory: A Century of Motor Racing*. Jersey City, N.J.: Parkwest Publications, 1994.

Stephenson, Sallie. *Race Cars*. Mankato, Minn.: Capstone Press, 1991.

Useful Addresses

NASCAR
P.O. Box 2875
Daytona Beach, FL 32120

Indianapolis Motor Speedway
4790 West 16th Street
Indianapolis, IN 46222

United States Automobile Club
4910 West 16th Street
Indianapolis, IN 46224

Canadian Automobile Sports Clubs
693 Petrolia Road
Downsview, ON M3J 2N6
Canada

Index

Alfa Romeo, 15, 35

Bentley, 15
Bonneville Salt Flats, 23
Brickyard, 27, 31
British Racing Motors, 35
Bugatti, 15

Charron, Fernand, 10
Cooper, Charles, 35
Cosworth, 35

Darlingon Beach, 25
Daytona Beach, 23, 24
Daytona 500, 24

Federation Internationale de
    l'Automobile, 33
Ferrari, 35
Ford, Henry, 23
France, Bill, 24

Grand National Series, 25

Harroun, Ray, 15

Indianapolis 500, 14, 15, 27, 28,
    29, 34
Indianapolis Motor Speedway, 14

Le Mans, 13, 42
Levassor, Emile, 9, 10

Lotus, 35

Marion, Milt, 24
Marmon Wasp, 15
Maserati, 15, 35
McLaren, 35
Mercedes, 15, 35
Miller, Harry, 28, 29
Miller 122, 28, 29
Monte Carlo, 37

Narragansett Park, 13
NASCAR, 24, 25
North Wilkesboro, 24

Offenhauser, Fred, 29

Panhard, 9

Renault, 35

Szisz, Ferenc, 13

Talbot, 35
Trans-Am Championship, 43

Vanwall, 35

Winston Cup Series, 25
World Championship, 34, 35
World of Outlaws, 40